Paper Snowflakes
For the Whole Family

Robert P. Kelley

Just Write Publishing Co.
©2022 All rights reserved.
ISBN 978-0-578-29331-8

00 Year Old Paper Snowflakes?

e Polish have the world's first tradition of making paper snowflakes. Their designs could have repeating imal, flower, and geometric shapes in them. They were usually more square-shaped than round. German rcular Valentines came next in the evolution of the paper snowflake. Young men would lovingly cut out ricate designs and write romantic poetry in the center of them. Bashful guys would ask for dates and even pose marriage. These Valentines were so special that their sweethearts treasured them. This was such a good a that it spawned an entire greeting card industry.

greater Europe, paper napkin folding and cutting flourished among the cultured elite. These lacy table napkins re status symbols of refined manners because the full compliment of silverware hadn't come into use yet. By early 1800's a London draper named Doiley popularized a cotton version of these decorative table napkins. ey eventually morphed into the modern doily. Today it's not a napkin at all, but an ornamental placemat.

e popular use of doilies has been fading in England because it is viewed as snobby and pompous, but they main so admired to some folks that a countermovement has started, "Save Our Doilies!" Paper snowflakes ke delightful doilies for memorable meals, and are wonderful for white weddings. They look brilliant with ng, and glamorous with glitter. Express your gentility and cultured refinement: Save Our Doilies!

eck the Halls with ... Paper Snowflakes!

king paper snowflakes is a perfect winter and holiday activity. Now everyone from age 3 to us BIG KIDS can ke paper snowflakes with a variety of festive designs for every skill level. Cozy up by the fireplace on those g cold winter nights. Invite your friends, family and neighbors over to join in the fun. Have a paper snowflake ty to decorate for the holidays! It's also a great "snow day" group activity for church, Girl Scouts, day care, and me school. Making paper snowflakes are a favorite activity for teachers and children as they help develop d-eye coordination and fine motor skills. Scissors are one of the first real tools children learn to utilize. There raises awareness of safety and how to work with tools properly. (Young children age 3 to 5 need adult pervision) Paper folding and cutting are so important to developing young minds that they are taught in ool in Japan as Kirigami (kir-i-**gah**-mee).

igami is even therapeutic and meditative like Origami (awr-i-**gah**-mee) can be. Kids learn the value of ience, precision, and practice. It's a relaxing and low stress way to focus the mind, but with tangible results. e kids get immediate rewards after they fold and cut the snowflakes out. They get to open presents. Little rks of art magically appear as they unfold them. Their faces beam with pride, "WOW! I made that!" Now even schoolers can make beautiful paper snowflakes like their older siblings. Cutting out repeating folded patterns o intrinsically satisfying it's not surprising that making paper snowflakes is perennially popular. Make them r after year after year … for every generation of your extended family.

Older Children, Adults, and Teachers

If you are new to this folk art, start with the 2 folds/4 sections snowflakes so that you can do all of the fold patterns. It's EZ PZ to learn if you do it progressively. If you are having concerns back down a level for awhile. patient, it will come. Practice makes perfect! After kids make all the snowflakes at their age level, they will be a to do the next age level up. This is a nice confidence boost. "I'm only six years old but I can do Age 7!" This i stark contrast to others paper snowflake books which are frustrating, if not impossible, for children to make.

Paper Folding and Cutting Tips

Do all paper folding with clean hands, on a clean, dry, hard, smooth surface. Carefully go over every fold wi fingernail or thumbnail. Try to fold and cut exactly on the guidelines. Take your time. Each folding pattern recommendations for paper weights that work best with it. Experiment with colored papers to match your de Vary the sizes of the snowflakes by reducing them. To enlarge them you will need larger paper.

While school or household scissors are all that you need, it is very important that they fit your hands, and are dull. Fiskars has reasonably priced quality scissors for every age group and hand size. Stock up, they will used. However, please be careful when using scissors, they can poke and bite. Don't run with scissors! Yo children need supervision.

For cutting curves and finer work, cut slowly and take small bites using the inside center of the scissor bla Don't "chase" the paper with your scissors. Hold your scissors steady and guide the paper into them with y other hand. It's easiest to cut from a fold or outside edge inwards. If you are right-handed, make the right side first, then the left. Work towards the left unless you are cutting out something like a circle or heart. Then w from the bottom of the cut up towards the right around the curve. Tightly hold the paper layers right next to y scissor blades. Find what works best for you. Remember to keep a waste basket close by for the little cut pie or you might get snowed in!

Displaying Your Snowflakes

Press the finished snowflakes flat under some books overnight. Tape them to clean windows with clear tape hang from the ceiling for a festive seasonal display from before Thanksgiving to after New Year's, or depend on your climate, from Halloween to Valentine's Day, even Easter.

Not all paper snowflakes hang well. Glue the more fragile ones to both sides of a 8" or 9" circle cut fi construction or card stock paper using small dots of glue. Hang them individually, or in snowmobile chain three or more. It's relaxing to watch them drift slowly to the imperceptible drafts of a still room … Laminat frame your favorites for years of use. Give them away as gifts. Decorate the office. "Look at what my little ge did!" Your co-workers will be envious. Make up your own winter wonderland!

PAPER SNOWFLAKES For the Whole Family

Do NOT cut pages out of book

Age 3
Cutouts

Photocopy page.
Cut out square.
Cut out circle.
Cut out snowflake.

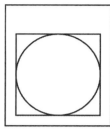 

Paper: 20# (75 gsm)
to 65# construction
paper (100 gsm).

Practice on 1 and
2 first. They
are easier.

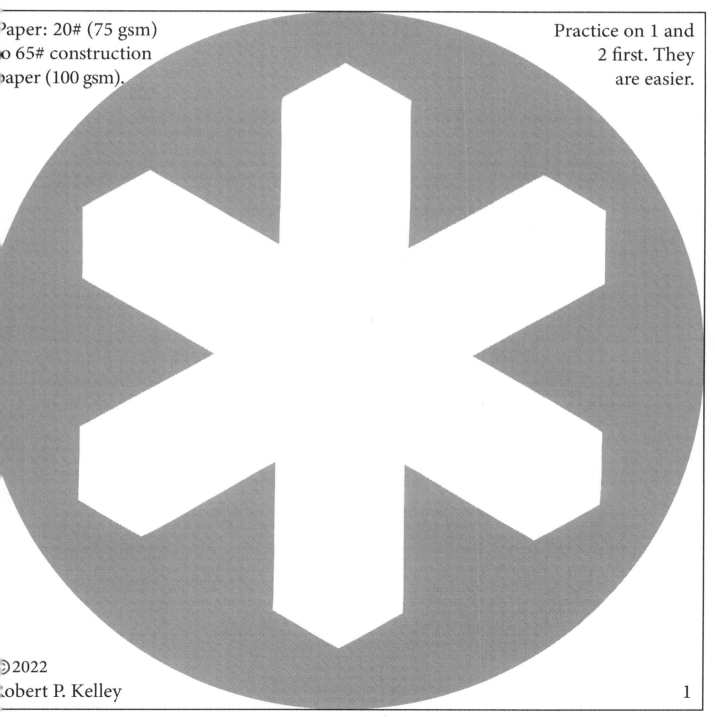

PAPER SNOWFLAKES For the Whole Family

Do NOT cut pages out of book

Ag[e]
Cuto[ut]

Photocopy page.
Cut out square.
Cut out circle.
Cut out snowflake.

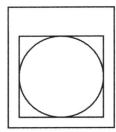

Paper: 20# (75 gsm) to 65# construction paper (100 gsm).

Practice on 1 an[d] 2 first. The[y] are easie[r]

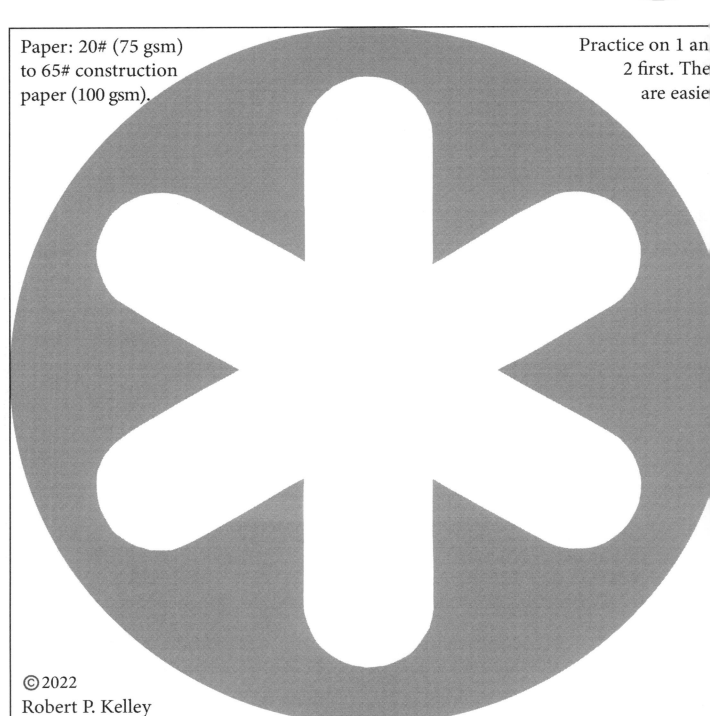

hotocopy page.
ut out square.
ut out circle.
ut out snowflake.

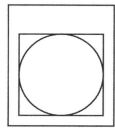

Try colored
papers.

Try to cut right
on the lines.

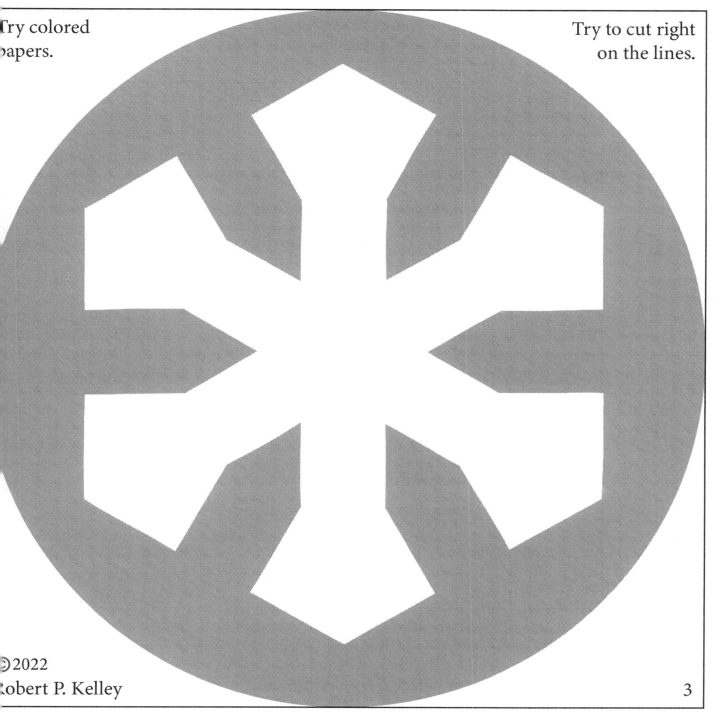

PAPER SNOWFLAKES For the Whole Family

Do NOT cut pages out of book

Age
Cutou

Photocopy page.
Cut out square.
Cut out circle.
Cut out snowflake.

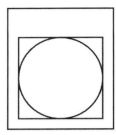

Paper: 20# (75 gsm)
to 65# construction
paper (100 gsm).

Be careful with scissor
They can pok
and bit

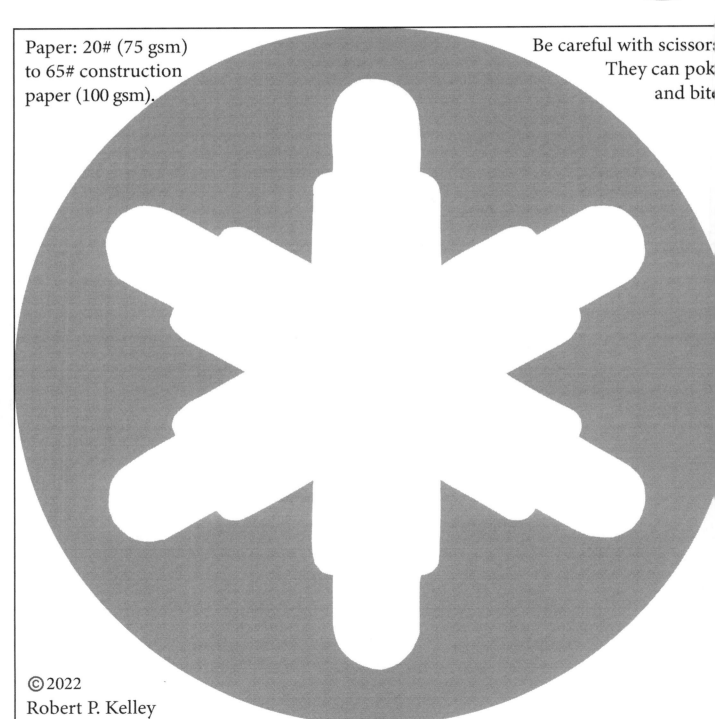

otocopy page.
ıt out square.
ıt out circle.
ıt out snowflake.

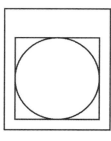

Paper: 20# (75 gsm)
o 65# construction
aper (100 gsm).

Be patient. Make
your very best
effort.

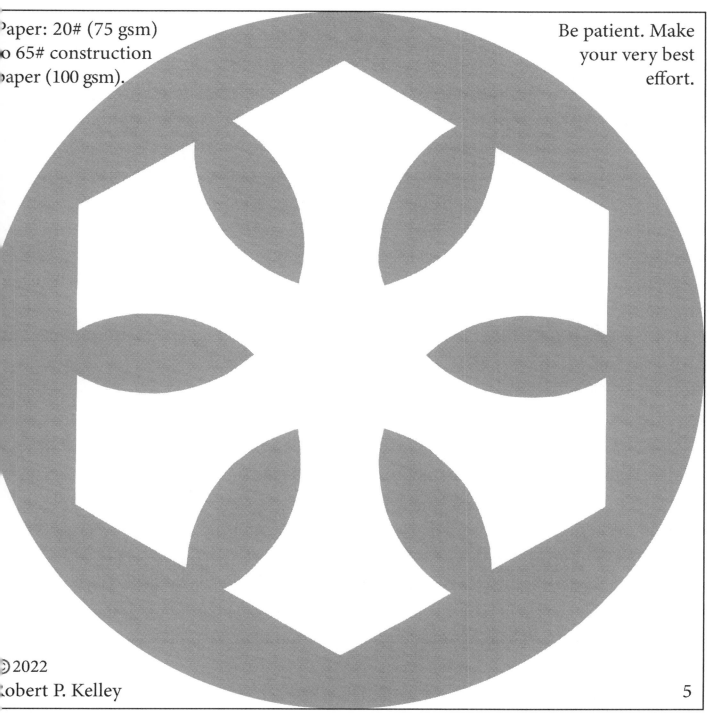

PAPER SNOWFLAKES For the Whole Family

Do NOT cut pages out of book

Photocopy page.
Cut out square.
Cut out circle.
Cut out snowflake.

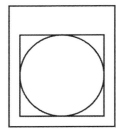
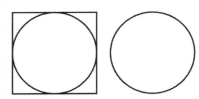

Try colored
papers.

Don't worry abou
mistakes. Ever
snowflake
differen

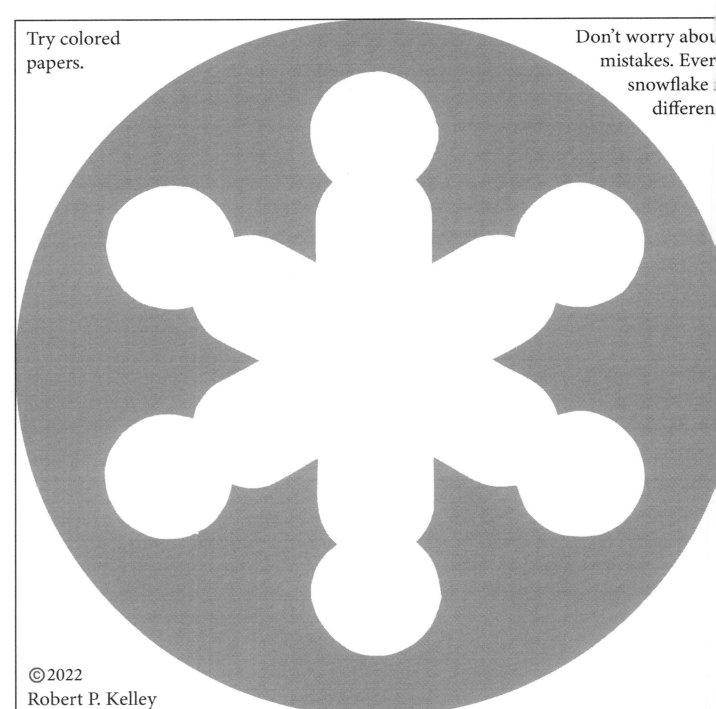

hotocopy page.
ut out square.
ut out circle.
ut out snowflake.

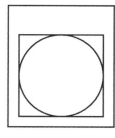

Paper: 20# (75 gsm)
o 65# construction
paper (100 gsm).

Practice makes
perfect.

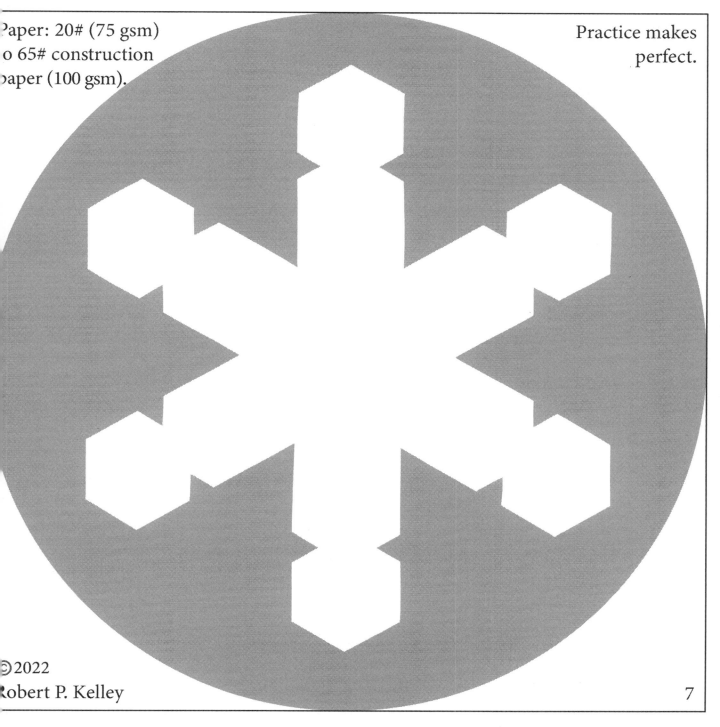

PAPER SNOWFLAKES For the Whole Family

Age
Cutou

Photocopy page.
Cut out square.
Cut out circle.
Cut out snowflake.

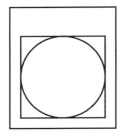

Paper: 20# (75 gsm)
to 65# construction
paper (100 gsm).

Do 8 and 9 las
They are mor
challenging

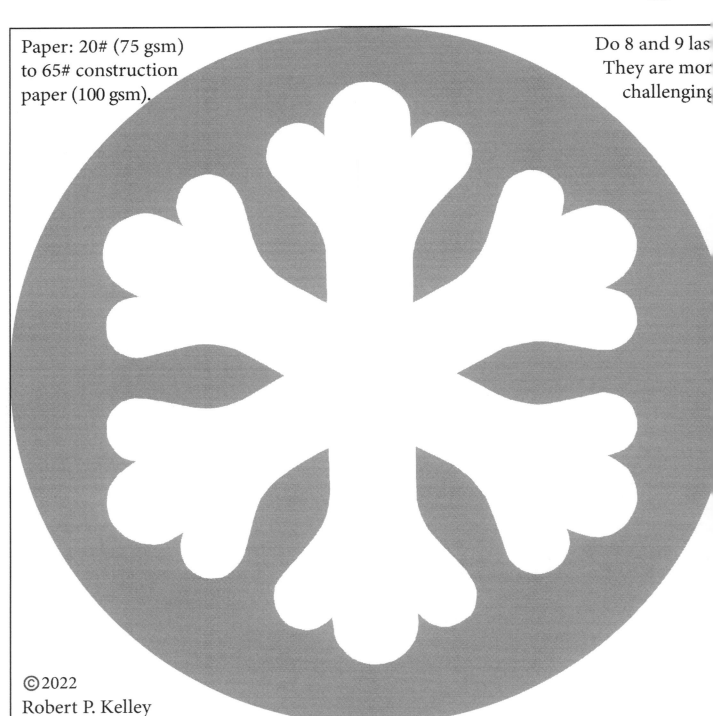

hotocopy page.
ut out square.
ut out circle.
ut out snowflake.

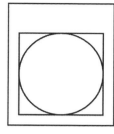 

ry colored
apers.

When you can do
all of Age 3,
try Age 4.

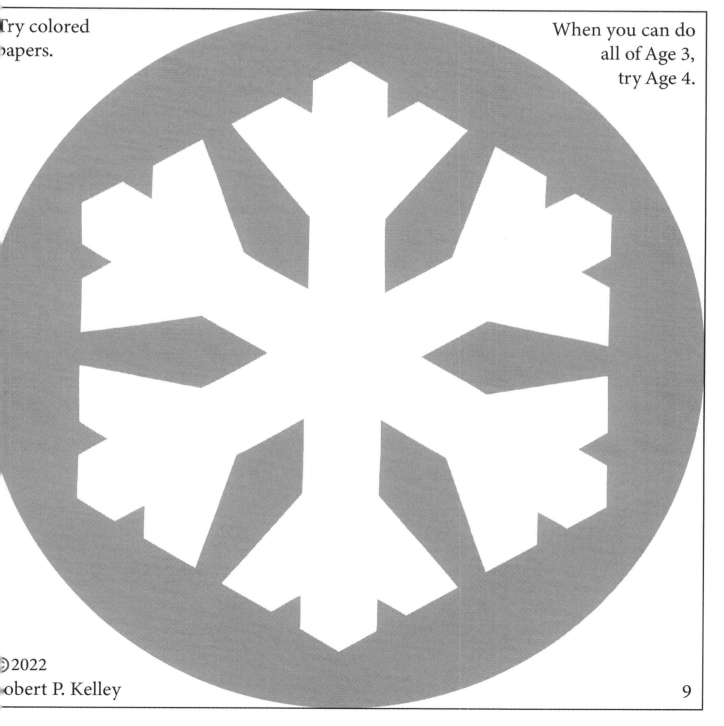

PAPER SNOWFLAKES For the Whole Family

Do NOT cut pages out of book

Photocopy page.
Cut out square.
Fold in half.
Cut out half circle.
Cut out gray area.

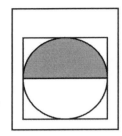   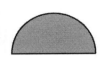 

Paper: 20# (75 gsm)
to 28# (105 gsm).

Practice on 10 an
11 first. The
are easie

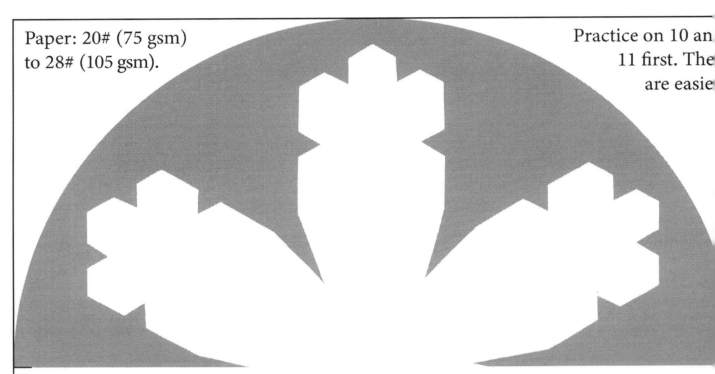

1

o NOT cut pages out of book

otocopy page.
it out square.
ld in half.
it out half circle.
it out gray area.

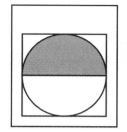

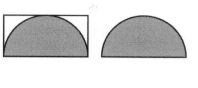

Paper: 20# (75 gsm)
o 28# (105 gsm).

Practice on 10 and
11 first. They
are easier.

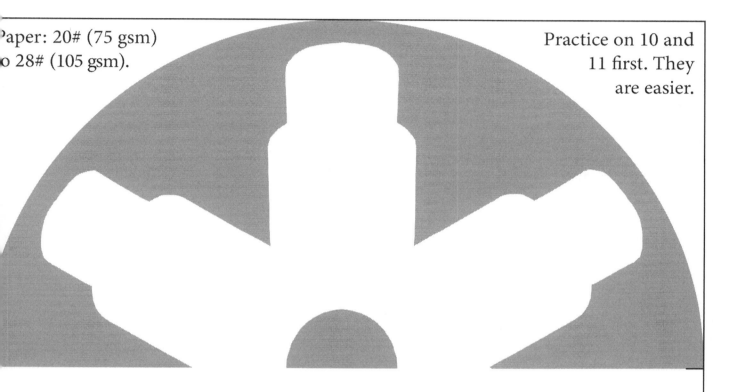

obert P. Kelley

PAPER SNOWFLAKES For the Whole Family

Do NOT cut pages out of book

Photocopy page.
Cut out square.
Fold in half.
Cut out half circle.
Cut out gray area.

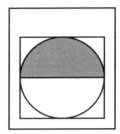

Try colored
papers.

Try to fold and cu
right on th
line

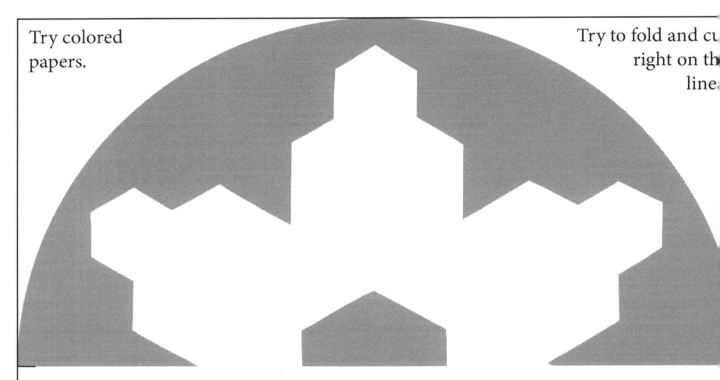

1

hotocopy page.
ut out square.
old in half.
ut out half circle.
ut out gray area.

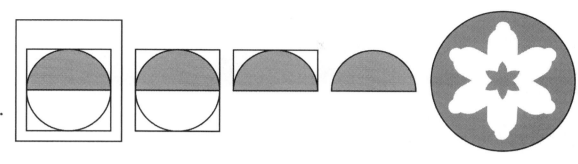

Paper: 20# (75 gsm)
o 28# (105 gsm).

Be careful with scissors.
They can poke
and bite.

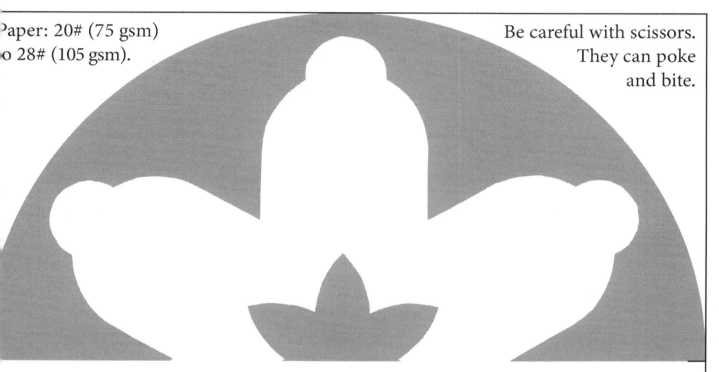

PAPER SNOWFLAKES For the Whole Family

Do NOT cut pages out of book

Photocopy page.
Cut out square.
Fold in half.
Cut out half circle.
Cut out gray area.

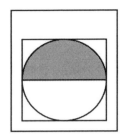

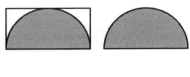
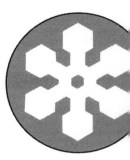

Paper: 20# (75 gsm)
to 28# (105 gsm).

Be patient. Mak
your very be
effor

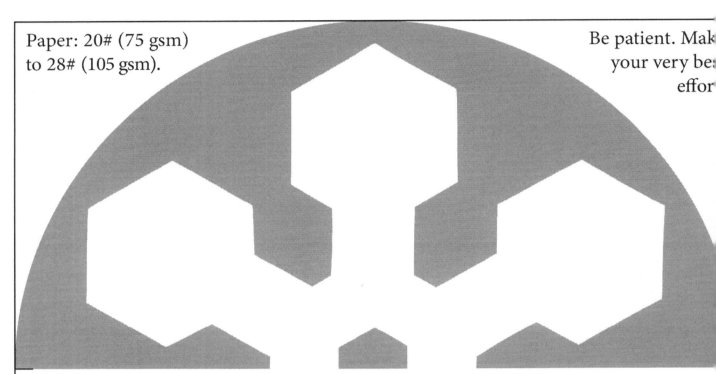

1

o NOT cut pages out of book

otocopy page.
t out square.
ld in half.
t out half circle.
t out gray area.

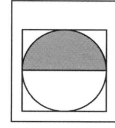

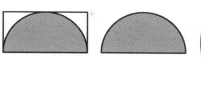

ry colored
apers.

Don't worry about
mistakes. Every
snowflake is
different.

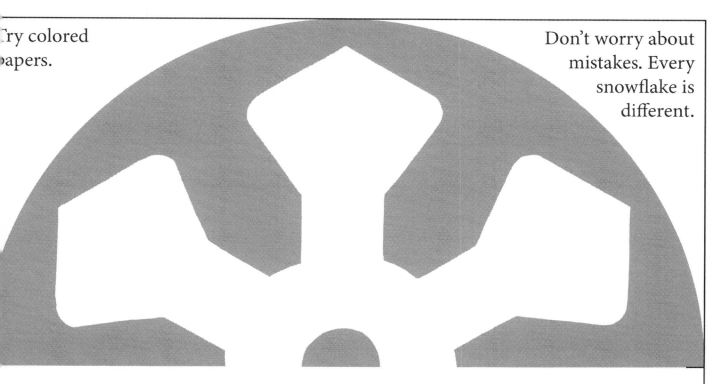

PAPER SNOWFLAKES For the Whole Family

Do NOT cut pages out of book

Photocopy page.
Cut out square.
Fold in half.
Cut out half circle.
Cut out gray area.

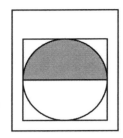 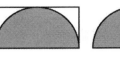 

Practice make
perfec

Paper: 20# (75 gsm)
to 28# (105 gsm).

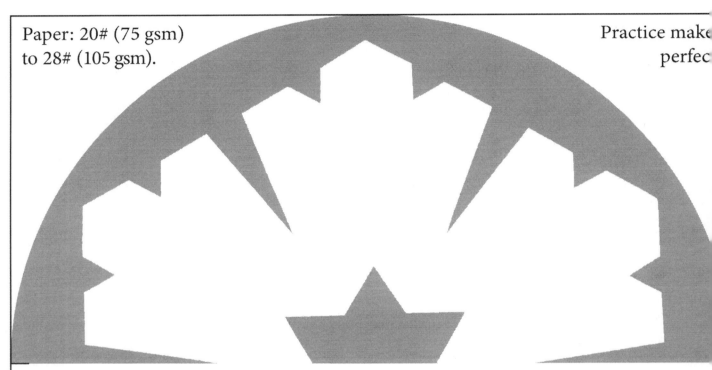

PAPER SNOWFLAKES For the Whole Family

o NOT cut pages out of book

Age 4
1 Fold, 2 Sections

hotocopy page.

ut out square.

ld in half.

ut out half circle.

ut out gray area.

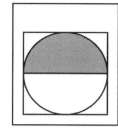    

Paper: 20# (75 gsm)
o 28# (105 gsm).

Do 17 and 18 last.
They are more
challenging.

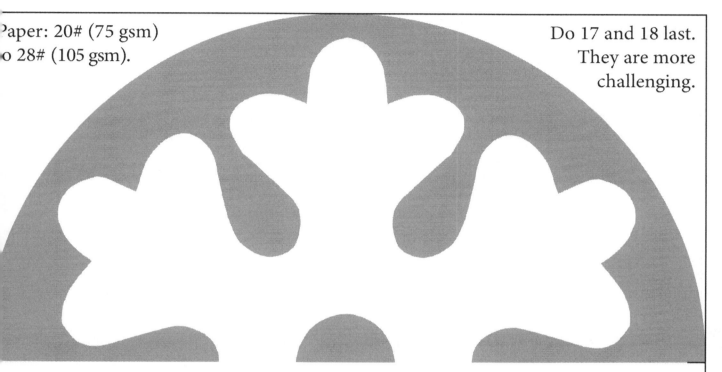

2022

Robert P. Kelley

17

PAPER SNOWFLAKES For the Whole Family

Do NOT cut pages out of book

Photocopy page.
Cut out square.
Fold in half.
Cut out half circle.
Cut out gray area.

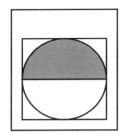 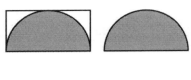 

Try colored
papers.

When you can d
all of Age
try Age

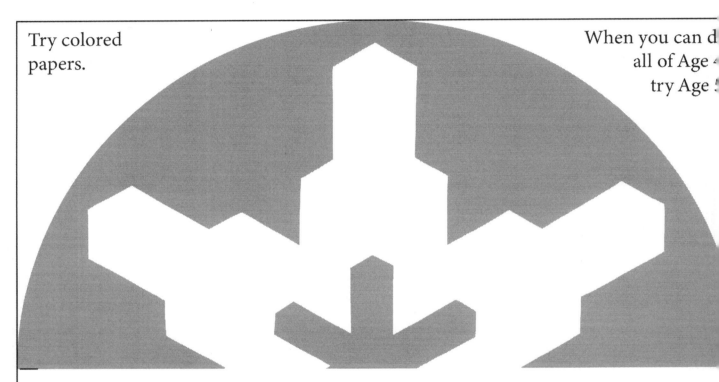

1

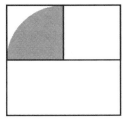 

Photocopy page. Cut out square.
Fold as shown. Cut off ends on
curve. Cut out gray areas. Unfold.

Paper: 20# (75 gsm)
o 24# (90 gsm).

Practice on 19 and
20 first. They
are easier.

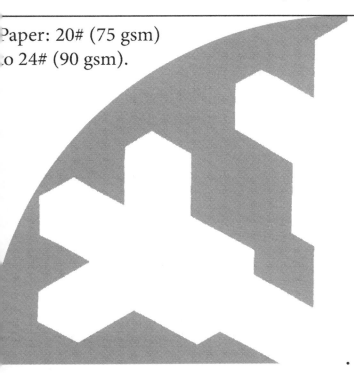

PAPER SNOWFLAKES For the Whole Family

Do NOT cut pages out of book

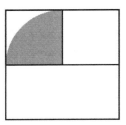 

Photocopy page. Cut out square.
Fold as shown. Cut off ends on
curve. Cut out gray areas. Unfold.

Paper: 20# (75 gsm)
to 24# (90 gsm).

Practice on 19 an
20 first. The
are easie

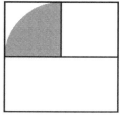 

Photocopy page. Cut out square.
Fold as shown. Cut off ends on
curve. Cut out gray areas. Unfold.

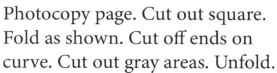

Try colored
papers.

Try to fold and cut
right on the
lines.

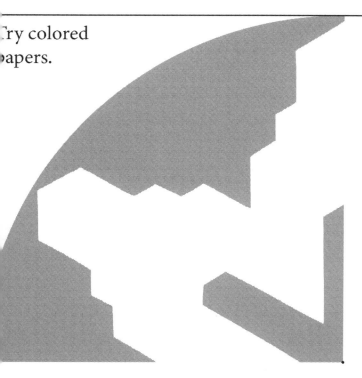

PAPER SNOWFLAKES For the Whole Family

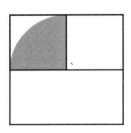 

Photocopy page. Cut out square.
Fold as shown. Cut off ends on
curve. Cut out gray areas. Unfold.

Paper: 20# (75 gsm)
to 24# (90 gsm).

Go over all fold
with a thumbna
or fingernai

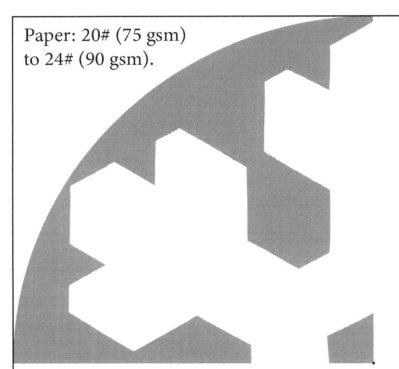

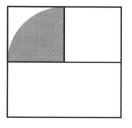 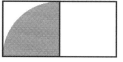

Photocopy page. Cut out square.
Fold as shown. Cut off ends on
curve. Cut out gray areas. Unfold.

Paper: 20# (75 gsm)
o 24# (90 gsm).

Be patient. Make
your very best
effort.

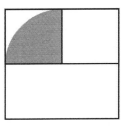 

Photocopy page. Cut out square.
Fold as shown. Cut off ends on
curve. Cut out gray areas. Unfold.

Try colored
papers.

Don't worry abou
mistakes. Ever
snowflake
differen

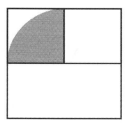 

Photocopy page. Cut out square.
Fold as shown. Cut off ends on
curve. Cut out gray areas. Unfold.

Paper: 20# (75 gsm)
o 24# (90 gsm).

Practice makes
perfect.

PAPER SNOWFLAKES For the Whole Family

Do NOT cut pages out of book

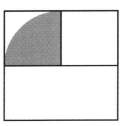 

Photocopy page. Cut out square. Fold as shown. Cut off ends on curve. Cut out gray areas. Unfold.

Do 26 and 27 las
They are mor
challenging

Paper: 20# (75 gsm) to 24# (90 gsm).

APER SNOWFLAKES For the Whole Family

Age 5

2 Folds, 4 Sections

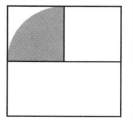 

Photocopy page. Cut out square. Fold as shown. Cut off ends on curve. Cut out gray areas. Unfold.

Try colored papers.

When you have made all of Age 5 templates, try Age 6.

©2022
Robert P. Kelley

27

PAPER SNOWFLAKES For the Whole Family

Do NOT cut pages out of book

 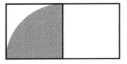

Photocopy page. Cut out square.
Fold as shown. Cut off ends on
curve. Cut out gray areas. Unfold.

Paper: 20# (75 gsm)
to 24# (90 gsm).

Practice on 28 an
29 first. The
are easie

2

APER SNOWFLAKES For the Whole Family

Age 6
2 Folds, 4 Sections

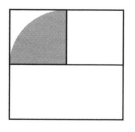 

Photocopy page. Cut out square.
Fold as shown. Cut off ends on
curve. Cut out gray areas. Unfold.

Paper: 20# (75 gsm)
o 24# (90 gsm).

Practice on 28 and
29 first. They
are easier.

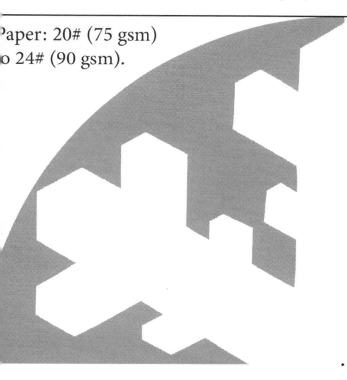

©2022
obert P. Kelley

29

PAPER SNOWFLAKES For the Whole Family

Do NOT cut pages out of book

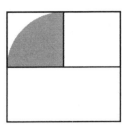 

Photocopy page. Cut out square.
Fold as shown. Cut off ends on
curve. Cut out gray areas. Unfold.

Try colored
papers.

Try to fold and cu
right on th
line

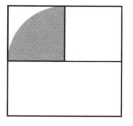 

Photocopy page. Cut out square.
Fold as shown. Cut off ends on
curve. Cut out gray areas. Unfold.

Paper: 20# (75 gsm)
to 24# (90 gsm).

Go over all folds
with a thumbnail
or fingernail.

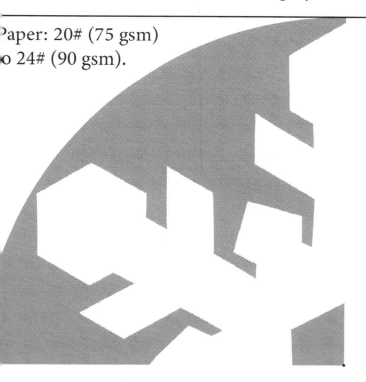

PAPER SNOWFLAKES For the Whole Family

Do NOT cut pages out of book

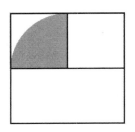 

Photocopy page. Cut out square.
Fold as shown. Cut off ends on
curve. Cut out gray areas. Unfold.

Be patient. Mak
your very be
effor

Paper: 20# (75 gsm)
to 24# (90 gsm).

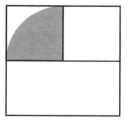 

Photocopy page. Cut out square.
Fold as shown. Cut off ends on
curve. Cut out gray areas. Unfold.

Try colored
papers.

Don't worry about
mistakes. Every
snowflake is
different.

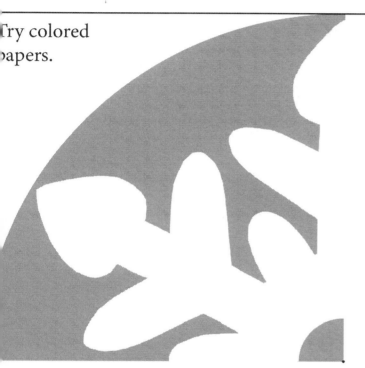

PAPER SNOWFLAKES For the Whole Family

Do NOT cut pages out of book

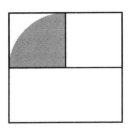 

Photocopy page. Cut out square.
Fold as shown. Cut off ends on
curve. Cut out gray areas. Unfold.

Practice make
perfec

Paper: 20# (75 gsm)
to 24# (90 gsm).

3

Photocopy page. Cut out square.
Fold as shown. Cut off ends on
curve. Cut out gray areas. Unfold.

Paper: 20# (75 gsm)
o 24# (90 gsm).

Do 35 and 36 last.
They are more
challenging.

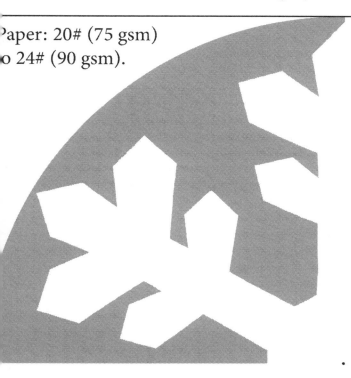

PAPER SNOWFLAKES For the Whole Family

Do NOT cut pages out of book

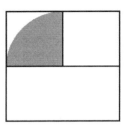 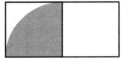

Photocopy page. Cut out square.
Fold as shown. Cut off ends on
curve. Cut out gray areas. Unfold.

Try colored
papers.

When you have made a
of Age 6 template
try Age

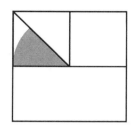 

Photocopy page. Cut out square.
Fold as shown. Cut off ends on
curve. Cut out gray areas. Unfold.

Paper: 20# (75 gsm).

Practice on 37 and
38 first. They
are easier.

PAPER SNOWFLAKES For the Whole Family

Do NOT cut pages out of book

Age
3 Folds, 8 Sectio

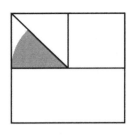 

Photocopy page. Cut out square.
Fold as shown. Cut off ends on
curve. Cut out gray areas. Unfold.

Paper: 20# (75 gsm).

Practice on 37 an
38 first. The
are easie

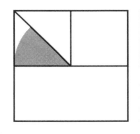

Photocopy page. Cut out square.
Fold as shown. Cut off ends on
curve. Cut out gray areas. Unfold.

Try colored
papers.

Try to fold and cut
right on the
lines.

PAPER SNOWFLAKES For the Whole Family

Do NOT cut pages out of book

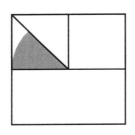  

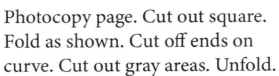

Photocopy page. Cut out square.
Fold as shown. Cut off ends on
curve. Cut out gray areas. Unfold.

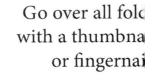

Go over all fold
with a thumbna
or fingerna

Paper: 20# (75 gsm).

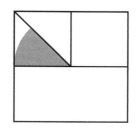 

Photocopy page. Cut out square.
Fold as shown. Cut off ends on
curve. Cut out gray areas. Unfold.

Paper: 20# (75 gsm)

Be patient. Make
your very best
effort.

© 2022
Robert P. Kelley

PAPER SNOWFLAKES For the Whole Family

Age

3 Folds, 8 Sectio

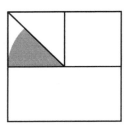 

Photocopy page. Cut out square.
Fold as shown. Cut off ends on
curve. Cut out gray areas. Unfold.

Try colored
papers.

Don't worry abou
mistakes. Ever
snowflake i
differen

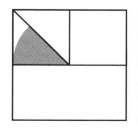 

Photocopy page. Cut out square.
Fold as shown. Cut off ends on
curve. Cut out gray areas. Unfold.

Paper: 20# (75 gsm).

Press your snowflakes
flat under some
books.

PAPER SNOWFLAKES For the Whole Family

Do NOT cut pages out of book

Age

3 Folds, 8 Sectio

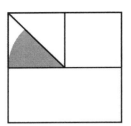  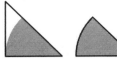

Photocopy page. Cut out square.
Fold as shown. Cut off ends on
curve. Cut out gray areas. Unfold.

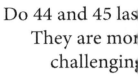

Paper: 20# (75 gsm).

Do 44 and 45 las
They are mor
challengin

© 2022
Robert P. Kelley

4

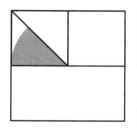    

Photocopy page. Cut out square.
Fold as shown. Cut off ends on
curve. Cut out gray areas. Unfold.

Try colored
papers.

When you have made all
of Age 7 templates,
try Age 8.

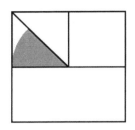

Photocopy page. Cut out square.
Fold as shown. Cut off ends on
curve. Cut out gray areas. Unfold.

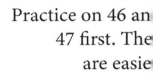

Paper: 20# (75 gsm).

Practice on 46 an
47 first. The
are easie

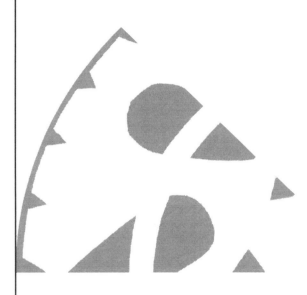

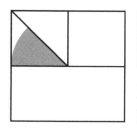 

Photocopy page. Cut out square.
Fold as shown. Cut off ends on
curve. Cut out gray areas. Unfold.

Paper: 20# (75 gsm).

Paper Doll Doily

PAPER SNOWFLAKES For the Whole Family

Do NOT cut pages out of book

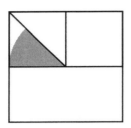  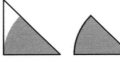

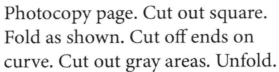

Photocopy page. Cut out square.
Fold as shown. Cut off ends on
curve. Cut out gray areas. Unfold.

Try colored
papers.

Try to fold and cu
right on th
line

4

PAPER SNOWFLAKES For the Whole Family

3 Folds, 8 Sections

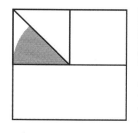 

Photocopy page. Cut out square.
Fold as shown. Cut off ends on
curve. Cut out gray areas. Unfold.

Paper: 20# (75 gsm).

Go over all folds
with a thumbnail
or fingernail.

PAPER SNOWFLAKES For the Whole Family

Do NOT cut pages out of book

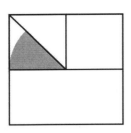  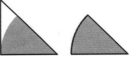

Photocopy page. Cut out square.
Fold as shown. Cut off ends on
curve. Cut out gray areas. Unfold.

Paper: 20# (75 gsm).

Be patient. Mak
your very be
effor

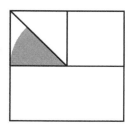

Photocopy page. Cut out square.
Fold as shown. Cut off ends on
curve. Cut out gray areas. Unfold.

Try colored
papers.

Use hole punch
around outside
edge.

PAPER SNOWFLAKES For the Whole Family

Do NOT cut pages out of book

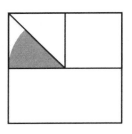  

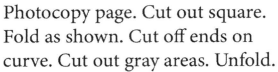

Photocopy page. Cut out square.
Fold as shown. Cut off ends on
curve. Cut out gray areas. Unfold.

Paper: 20# (75 gsm).

Hang your snowflake
from the ceilin

PAPER SNOWFLAKES For the Whole Family

Do NOT cut pages out of book

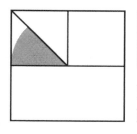    

Photocopy page. Cut out square. Fold as shown. Cut off ends on curve. Cut out gray areas. Unfold.

Paper: 20# (75 gsm).

Do 53 and 54 last. They are more challenging.

Do NOT cut pages out of book

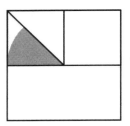 

Photocopy page. Cut out square.
Fold as shown. Cut off ends on
curve. Cut out gray areas. Unfold.

Paper: 20# (75 gsm).

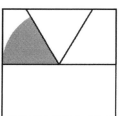 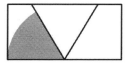  

Photocopy page. Cut out square. Fold as shown. Cut off ends on curve. Cut out gray areas. Unfold.

Paper: 20# (75 gsm) o 24# (90 gsm).

Practice on 55 and 56 first. They are easier.

PAPER SNOWFLAKES For the Whole Family

Do NOT cut pages out of book

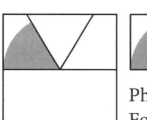 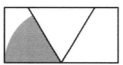 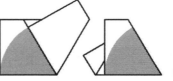 

Photocopy page. Cut out square.
Fold as shown. Cut off ends on
curve. Cut out gray areas. Unfold.

Paper: 20# (75 gsm)
to 24# (90 gsm).

Practice on 55 an
56 first. The
are easie

Age 9
3 Folds, 6 Sections

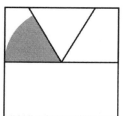 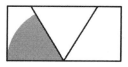 

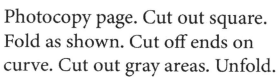

Photocopy page. Cut out square.
Fold as shown. Cut off ends on
curve. Cut out gray areas. Unfold.

Try colored
papers.

Try to fold and cut
right on the
lines.

©2022
Robert P. Kelley

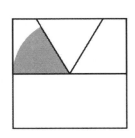 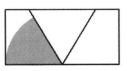 

Photocopy page. Cut out square.
Fold as shown. Cut off ends on
curve. Cut out gray areas. Unfold.

Paper: 20# (75 gsm)
to 24# (90 gsm).

Go over all fold
with a thumbna
or fingernai

o NOT cut pages out of book

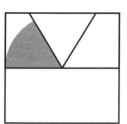 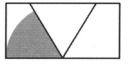 

Photocopy page. Cut out square.
Fold as shown. Cut off ends on
curve. Cut out gray areas. Unfold.

Paper: 20# (75 gsm)
o 24# (90 gsm).

Be patient. Make
your very best
effort.

Robert P. Kelley

Do NOT cut pages out of book

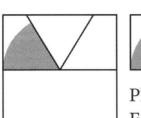 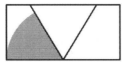  

Photocopy page. Cut out square. Fold as shown. Cut off ends on curve. Cut out gray areas. Unfold.

Try colored papers.

Don't worry abou mistakes. Ever snowflake differen

APER SNOWFLAKES For the Whole Family

Age 9

3 Folds, 6 Sections

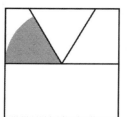 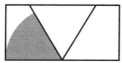  

Photocopy page. Cut out square.
Fold as shown. Cut off ends on
curve. Cut out gray areas. Unfold.

Paper: 20# (75 gsm)
o 24# (90 gsm).

Tape your snowflakes
to the windows.

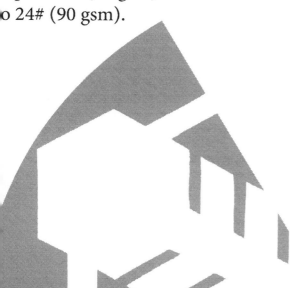

PAPER SNOWFLAKES For the Whole Family

Do NOT cut pages out of book

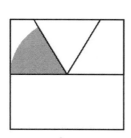 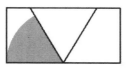 

Photocopy page. Cut out square.
Fold as shown. Cut off ends on
curve. Cut out gray areas. Unfold.

Paper: 20# (75 gsm)
to 24# (90 gsm).

Snowflakes are Dancin

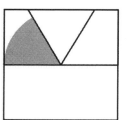 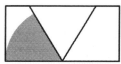  

Photocopy page. Cut out square.
Fold as shown. Cut off ends on
curve. Cut out gray areas. Unfold.

Try colored
papers.

When you have made all
of Age 9 templates,
try Age 10.

PAPER SNOWFLAKES For the Whole Family

Do NOT cut pages out of book

Age

3 Folds, 6 Sectio

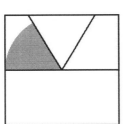 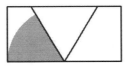 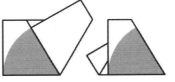 

Photocopy page. Cut out square.
Fold as shown. Cut off ends on
curve. Cut out gray areas. Unfold.

Paper: 20# (75 gsm)
to 24# (90 gsm).

Practice on 64 an
65 first. The
are easie

©2022
Robert P. Kelley

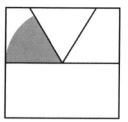 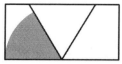 

Photocopy page. Cut out square.
Fold as shown. Cut off ends on
curve. Cut out gray areas. Unfold.

Paper: 20# (75 gsm)
to 24# (90 gsm).

Practice on 64 and
65 first. They
are easier.

PAPER SNOWFLAKES For the Whole Family

Do NOT cut pages out of book

Age

3 Folds, 6 Section

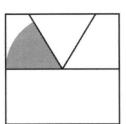 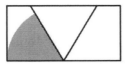  

Photocopy page. Cut out square.
Fold as shown. Cut off ends on
curve. Cut out gray areas. Unfold.

Try Origami
papers.

Try to fold and cu
right on th
line

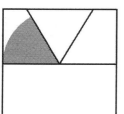 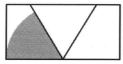 

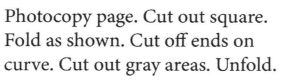

Photocopy page. Cut out square. Fold as shown. Cut off ends on curve. Cut out gray areas. Unfold.

Paper: 20# (75 gsm) to 24# (90 gsm).

Baron's Snowflake

PAPER SNOWFLAKES For the Whole Family

Do NOT cut pages out of book

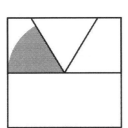 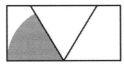 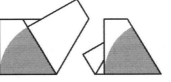 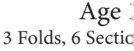 

Photocopy page. Cut out square.
Fold as shown. Cut off ends on
curve. Cut out gray areas. Unfold.

Paper: 20# (75 gsm)
to 24# (90 gsm).

Be patient. Mak
your very be.
effor

6

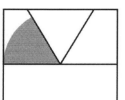 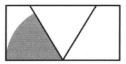  

Photocopy page. Cut out square.
Fold as shown. Cut off ends on
curve. Cut out gray areas. Unfold.

Try Origami
papers.

Around the World
Doily

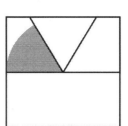 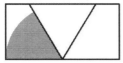  

Photocopy page. Cut out square.
Fold as shown. Cut off ends on
curve. Cut out gray areas. Unfold.

For finer work, cu
slowly and tak
small bite

Paper: 20# (75 gsm)
to 24# (90 gsm).

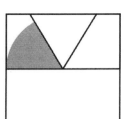 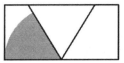  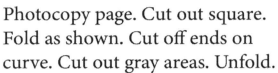

Photocopy page. Cut out square.
Fold as shown. Cut off ends on
curve. Cut out gray areas. Unfold.

Paper: 20# (75 gsm)
to 24# (90 gsm).

Angels and Candles

PAPER SNOWFLAKES For the Whole Family

Do NOT cut pages out of book

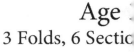

Age

3 Folds, 6 Sectio

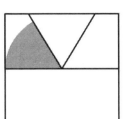 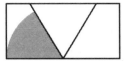 

Photocopy page. Cut out square. Fold as shown. Cut off ends on curve. Cut out gray areas. Unfold.

Try Origami papers.

Buddha and th
Bodhi Tre

o NOT cut pages out of book

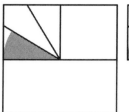

Photocopy page. Cut out square.
Fold as shown. Cut off ends on
curve. Cut out gray areas. Unfold.

Paper: 18# (64 gsm)
o 20# (75 gsm).

Practice on 73 and
74 first. They
are easier.

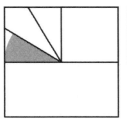 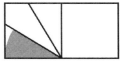 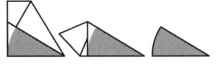 

Photocopy page. Cut out square.
Fold as shown. Cut off ends on
curve. Cut out gray areas. Unfold.

Paper: 18# (64 gsm)
to 20# (75 gsm).

Practice on 73 an
74 first. The
are easie

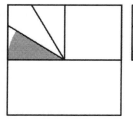 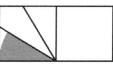 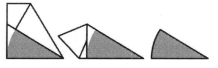

Photocopy page. Cut out square.
Fold as shown. Cut off ends on
curve. Cut out gray areas. Unfold.

ry colored
apers.

Try to fold and cut
exactly on the
lines.

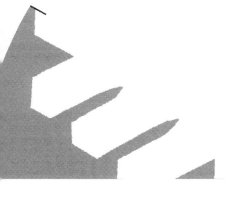

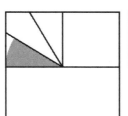 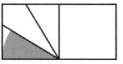 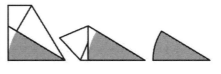 

Photocopy page. Cut out square.
Fold as shown. Cut off ends on
curve. Cut out gray areas. Unfold.

Paper: 18# (64 gsm)
to 20# (75 gsm).

Go over all fol
with a thumbna
or fingerna

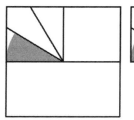

Photocopy page. Cut out square.
Fold as shown. Cut off ends on
curve. Cut out gray areas. Unfold.

Paper: 18# (64 gsm)
o 20# (75 gsm).

Put 2 staples in
the areas to
be cut out.

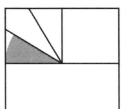 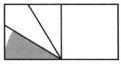 

Photocopy page. Cut out square.
Fold as shown. Cut off ends on
curve. Cut out gray areas. Unfold.

Try colored
papers.

Be patient. Mak
your very be
effor

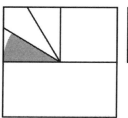
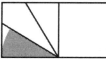

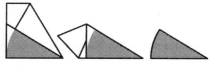
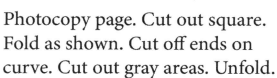

Photocopy page. Cut out square.
Fold as shown. Cut off ends on
curve. Cut out gray areas. Unfold.

Paper: 18# (64 gsm)
to 20# (75 gsm).

Practice makes
perfect.

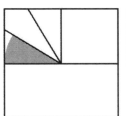 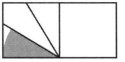 

Photocopy page. Cut out square.
Fold as shown. Cut off ends on
curve. Cut out gray areas. Unfold.

Paper: 18# (64 gsm)
to 20# (75 gsm).

Do 80 and 81 las
They are mor
challengin

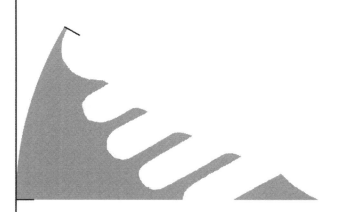

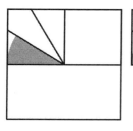  

Photocopy page. Cut out square.
Fold as shown. Cut off ends on
curve. Cut out gray areas. Unfold.

ry colored
apers.

When you have made all
of Age 11 templates,
try Age 12+.

2022

obert P. Kelley

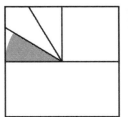 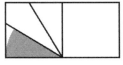 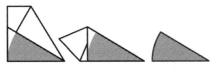 

Photocopy page. Cut out square.
Fold as shown. Cut off ends on
curve. Cut out gray areas. Unfold.

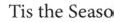

Paper: 18# (64 gsm)
to 20# (75 gsm).

Tis the Seaso

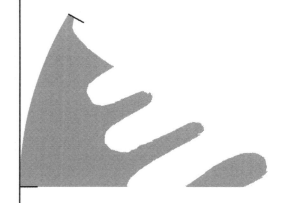

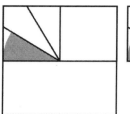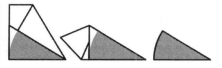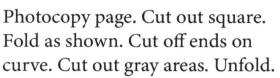

Photocopy page. Cut out square.
Fold as shown. Cut off ends on
curve. Cut out gray areas. Unfold.

~~P~~aper: 18# (64 gsm)
~~t~~o 20# (75 gsm).

Practice on 82 and
83 first. They
are easier.

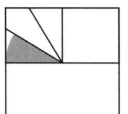 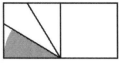 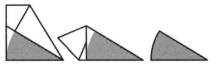 

Photocopy page. Cut out square.
Fold as shown. Cut off ends on
curve. Cut out gray areas. Unfold.

Try colored
papers.

Try to fold and cu
exactly on th
line.

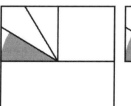  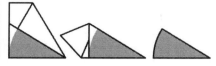 

Photocopy page. Cut out square.
Fold as shown. Cut off ends on
curve. Cut out gray areas. Unfold.

Paper: 18# (64 gsm)
o 20# (75 gsm).

Go over all folds
with a thumbnail
or fingernail.

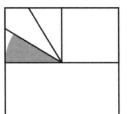  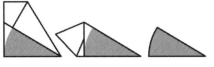

Photocopy page. Cut out square.
Fold as shown. Cut off ends on
curve. Cut out gray areas. Unfold.

Paper: 18# (64 gsm)
to 20# (75 gsm).

Put 2 staples i
the areas t
be cut ou

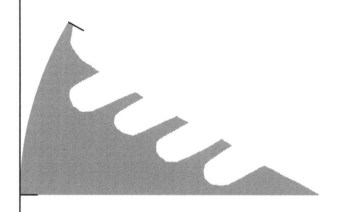

8

NOT cut pages out of book

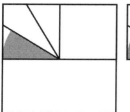   

Photocopy page. Cut out square.
Fold as shown. Cut off ends on
curve. Cut out gray areas. Unfold.

ry colored
apers.

Be patient. Make
your very best
effort.

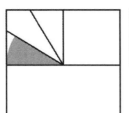 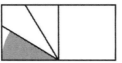 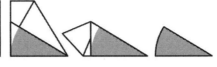 

Photocopy page. Cut out square.
Fold as shown. Cut off ends on
curve. Cut out gray areas. Unfold.

Paper: 18# (64 gsm)
to 20# (75 gsm).

Practice mak
perfec

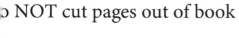
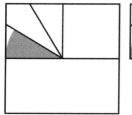
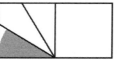

Photocopy page. Cut out square.
Fold as shown. Cut off ends on
curve. Cut out gray areas. Unfold.

Paper: 18# (64 gsm)
20# (75 gsm).

Snowbirds

2022
obert P. Kelley

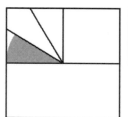  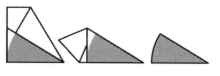 

Photocopy page. Cut out square.
Fold as shown. Cut off ends on
curve. Cut out gray areas. Unfold.

Try colored
papers.

When you have made a
of Age 12+ template
try Adul

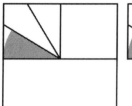 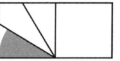 

Photocopy page. Cut out square.
Fold as shown. Cut off ends on
curve. Cut out gray areas. Unfold.

Paper: 18# (64 gsm)
o 20# (75 gsm).

Practice on 91 and
92 first. They
are easier.

Do NOT cut pages out of book

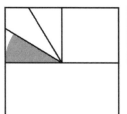 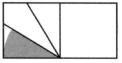 

Photocopy page. Cut out square.
Fold as shown. Cut off ends on
curve. Cut out gray areas. Unfold.

Paper: 18# (64 gsm)
to 20# (75 gsm).

Practice on 91 an
92 first. The
are easie

9

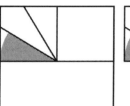   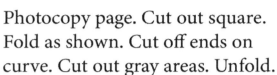

Photocopy page. Cut out square.
Fold as shown. Cut off ends on
curve. Cut out gray areas. Unfold.

ry Origami
apers.

Try to fold and cut
exactly on the
lines.

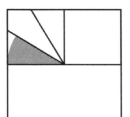 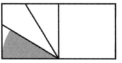  

Photocopy page. Cut out square.
Fold as shown. Cut off ends on
curve. Cut out gray areas. Unfold.

Paper: 18# (64 gsm)
to 20# (75 gsm).

Go over all fold
with a thumbna
or fingernai

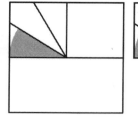

Photocopy page. Cut out square.
Fold as shown. Cut off ends on
curve. Cut out gray areas. Unfold.

Paper: 18# (64 gsm)
20# (75 gsm).

Put 2 staples in
the areas to
be cut out.

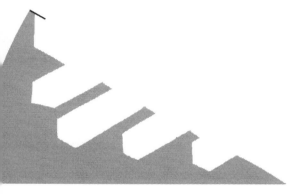

2022

obert P. Kelley

PAPER SNOWFLAKES For the Whole Family

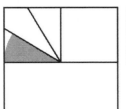   

Photocopy page. Cut out square.
Fold as shown. Cut off ends on
curve. Cut out gray areas. Unfold.

Try Origami
papers.

Be patient. Mal
your very be
effor

...o NOT cut pages out of book

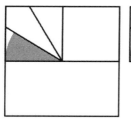  

Photocopy page. Cut out square.
Fold as shown. Cut off ends on
curve. Cut out gray areas. Unfold.

...aper: 18# (64 gsm)
...o 20# (75 gsm).

Practice makes
perfect.

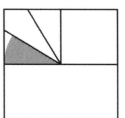 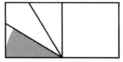 

Photocopy page. Cut out square.
Fold as shown. Cut off ends on
curve. Cut out gray areas. Unfold.

Paper: 18# (64 gsm)
to 20# (75 gsm).

Do 98 and 99 las
They are mor
challengin

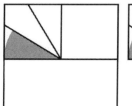  

Photocopy page. Cut out square.
Fold as shown. Cut off ends on
curve. Cut out gray areas. Unfold.

'ry Origami
apers.

When you have made all
of Adult templates,
try Advanced.

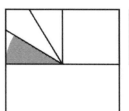 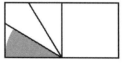 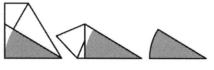

Photocopy page. Cut out square.
Fold as shown. Cut off ends on
curve. Cut out gray areas. Unfold.

Paper: 18# (64 gsm)
to 20# (75 gsm).

For Princess Dian

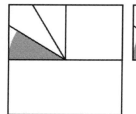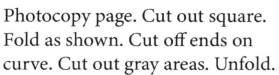

Photocopy page. Cut out square.
Fold as shown. Cut off ends on
curve. Cut out gray areas. Unfold.

Paper: 18# (64 gsm)
20# (75 gsm).

Crystal Crest

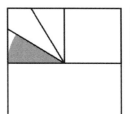  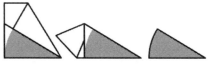

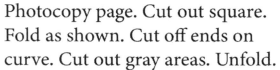

Photocopy page. Cut out square.
Fold as shown. Cut off ends on
curve. Cut out gray areas. Unfold.

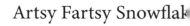

Honest reviews are
appreciated.

Artsy Fartsy Snowflak

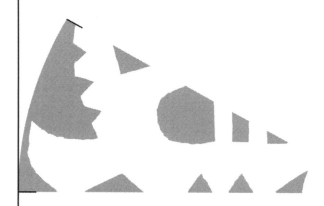

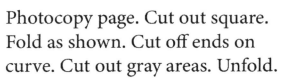

Photocopy page. Cut out square.
Fold as shown. Cut off ends on
curve. Cut out gray areas. Unfold.

Paper: 18# (64 gsm)
o 20# (75 gsm).

Hommage to MC Escher

PAPER SNOWFLAKES For the Whole Family

Do NOT cut pages out of book

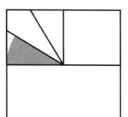  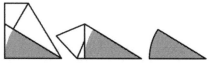

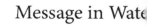

Photocopy page. Cut out square.
Fold as shown. Cut off ends on
curve. Cut out gray areas. Unfold.

Paper: 18# (64 gsm)
to 20# (75 gsm).

Message in Wate

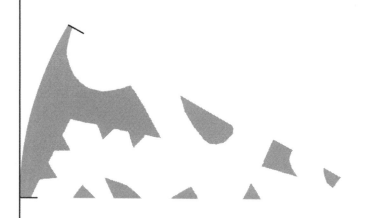

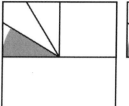  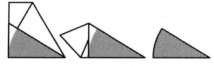

Photocopy page. Cut out square.
Fold as shown. Cut off ends on
curve. Cut out gray areas. Unfold.

Jse razor knife
nd pinking
hears.

Rocket Surgery

Do NOT cut pages out of book

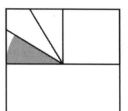  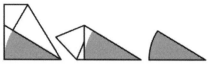 

Photocopy page. Cut out square.
Fold as shown. Cut off ends on
curve. Cut out gray areas. Unfold.

Use pinking
shears for
accents.

Aunt Pat's Cryst.

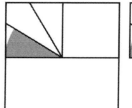  

Photocopy page. Cut out square.
Fold as shown. Cut off ends on
curve. Cut out gray areas. Unfold.

Paper: 18# (64 gsm)
to 20# (75 gsm).

Fern-like Crystal

©2022
Robert P. Kelley

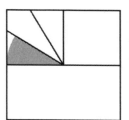 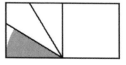 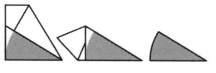 

Photocopy page. Cut out square.
Fold as shown. Cut off ends on
curve. Cut out gray areas. Unfold.

Try Origami
papers.

Mandala Snowflak

Made in the USA
Columbia, SC
12 November 2022

70928548R00063